The Risk
I Took

ISBN : 979-8-9936648-0-4

Written by Tyler Copple

Cover design and illustrations by Tyler Copple

Published by Tyler Copple

Special Thanks

To my aunt, Colette: Thank you for squinting through the rough draft, marking the margins, and pretending not to notice the emotional chaos tucked between the lines. You didn't just glance through the pages, you *studied* them. You gave this book more than just your time. You gave it your heart. And somehow, every note you made; every little tweak, every phrasing change, every whispered "what if"; brought this book closer to what it was meant to be. Your patience and honesty helped this book grow legs(and maybe a backbone).

And to Brook: Thank you for being the kind of friend who reads between the lines and still sticks around. Your suggestions may have been small, but your support was certainly anything but. I don't know if this book will go anywhere, but if it does, know that you helped it find its feet.

Also, just to be clear: reading drafts does not entitle you to royalties. You proofread a poetry book, you didn't cowrite Harry Potter. Let's all relax a little.

Seriously though, thank you for lending your hearts to these pages before the world ever saw them. I'll carry that forever.

Contents

Shadows   1

Emerald Eyes   2

The Glass Between Us   4

Unspoken   7

The Waiting Game   8

The Fall   9

The Miles Between   11

About To Meet You   12

Possibilities   14

Masterpiece   18

Already Yours   20

A Love So Divine   21

The Wizard   22

Tiger Lily   24

Quiet Realizations   27

Yellow   28

Crazy   30

A Prayer   31

Wake Of A Masterpiece   34

Almost   36

I Stayed   38

A Little Bit Yours   39

Still It Happened   40

Tattooed Heart   42

"Good night, Sleep well"   44

Glass Smile   45

I Lied   46

More Than This   49

Still Saying Good Night   50

Roses   52

Unbound   54

White Suit   55

Borrowed Book   56

Spoiled   58

The Gallery   62

Cracked   64

Her Own Flowers   65

Just A Memory   66

The Breeze   68

I Don't Need To Move On   70

Not Enough   71

The Echoes Between Us   72

I Showed Up   73

The Last Bag I'll Ever Pack   74

Walk Away   76

Can't Be Friends   78

The Risk I Took   79

The Risk I Took

A poetry collection where friendship and love collide.

Written and Illustrated by

Tyler Copple

Shadows

I've captured unicorns in flight
Through twilight's purple skies
Danced with Aphrodite
As I gazed into her eyes

I've been intrigued by whispering angels
Frozen by the breath of the divine
Made love atop soft silver clouds
Built castles from the sands of time

In a breath I've taken in
The scent of all that perfumes Eden
Bathed in glistening moonlight
Transformed rainbows into seasons

But mythic journeys through the heavens
Have never taken me as high
As the magic of her presence
Or the sparkle in her eyes

She is a goddess of love and beauty
Ethereal, yet refined
Enchanting as the blackest rose
Yet radiant as sunshine

She has the smile of an angel
A butterfly's gentle touch
Tis' she who mystifies my dreams
I've come to love so much

Forbidden love concealed in shadows
Haunting secrets unrevealed
Despair and sorrow fill my eyes
For She knows not, how I feel

Emerald Eyes

Her eyes, twin pools of emerald fire
A jungle vast, where dreams conspire
Vines of thought, weave trails unseen
Through worlds, both wild and serene

Within their depths, a river glides
A quiet current where wonder abides
You wander deep, a willing stray
Lost in her labyrinth, you choose to stay

For in her gaze, a forest lies
Alive beneath her Emerald Eyes

The Glass Between Us

I reach across the empty space
Fingers searching for something real
For the warmth that stories never held
For the touch that words can't quite deliver

Every step closer
Every breath slower
And still
The air stays thick
Like something unseen
Holding us apart

We speak in echoes
Send signals through screens
But the distance...
It waits there, patient and cold
Pretending not to be
A wall of glass between us

Clear, unyielding
Reflecting all we want
But never letting go

I want to shatter it
To break through the silence
To feel your hand in mine
Not just in dreams or text

But for now
We dance around the edges
Pretending the distance
Didn't feel like a glass wall between us

It began with the color.
A forest at dawn, wet with rain,
Yet in the shadows beneath
I found her laughter, her grief,
Her fire, her grace...
And I knew I'd never look away

Unspoken

I stand on the edge, a quiet plea
Eyes searching yours, but what do you see?
A heart that whispers, yet stays concealed
A love unspoken, a truth unrevealed

I wonder if you feel the same
Or if my heart is just a fleeting flame
In every glance, I search for clues
Trapped between your silent fingers

Do you notice the moments we share?
The way the world softens whenever you're there?
Or am I just a shadow in your light
A dream that fades with the passing night?

I don't know where this path may lead
But still, my heart dares to plead
If you could see what's hidden within
Perhaps we'd find where love begins

The Waiting Game

I wait in silence, heart in hand
Her footsteps soft upon the sand
The hours stretch like distant skies
As time reflects in longing eyes

Her laughter echoes in my mind
A melody so sweet, divine
I watch the stars, but none compare
To the spark of love we'll one day share

Her presence is the light I seek
A quiet strength, so soft, so sleek
And though the world springs on its way
I wait for her, come what may

In patience, love, and dreams so grand
I wait for her to take my hand
For in the pause, The Waiting Game
My life will never be the same

The Fall

We didn't mean to become everything
But somehow, we did
A call that never ended
Days stitched together with laughter and secrets
Told in the hush between yawns

FaceTime at 2 a.m.□
Your ceiling fan spinning behind you like a clock
That refused to end the night
We talked about nothing
About everything
About meeting one day...
And we both said "when", not "if"

It was easy
Like gravity
Like I'd known you in another life and we were just remembering
How to find each other again

We'd fall asleep with the screen still on
Your breath in rhythm with mine
Phones clutched like lifelines
Neither of us ready to let go
Even to dream

You became the first person I wanted to tell things to
The last voice I heard before sleep
My world, quietly
Started to echo your accent

We were still calling it friendship
But something unnamed was already growing
Quiet as a secret
Loud as a heartbeat

And suddenly
The fall didn't feel so far

Something is happening
A change is taking place
I've seen the way you look at me
Perceived the wonder in your gaze

I'm almost scared to take a breath
I somehow know you feel it too
Perhaps the stars conspired again
To place my orbit close to you

The Miles Between

Don't let the miles between us
Keep our love apart
Just listen close and you will hear
The beating of my heart

No distance will ever keep
My heart from loving you
There are no more tears for it to weep
For a love that runs so true

I'll be there with you one day soon
To love you everyday
And then my heart will sing a tune
And you will hear it say

I've finally found my one true love
As true as one can be
And now you're all I'm thinking of
Forever you and me

About To Meet You

It's almost time, and my pulse is a river
Rushing beneath calm skin
Breath catches, thoughts spin
And somewhere beneath it all
Your name hums
Like a song I'm afraid to end

I've held you in screens
In words that glowed blue at midnight
In dreams that felt too fragile
To say aloud

Now here we are...
Or almost
Almost real
Almost there

And still my heart plays what-ifs
What if I'm not what you hoped for
What if I fall and you don't reach back
What if this magic
Only lived in the space between

I've memorized your smile
From photos and laughter
But what if, face to face
You look at me
And see too much
Or not enough...

Yet even through the fears
Hope flickers
Delicate and defiant
Maybe this is it
Maybe it begins here
With shaking hands and brave steps
And the soft, slow bloom
Of something more

So I breathe and I brace
And I whisper a quiet prayer
To the version of me
That's about to meet you

Possibilities

I stood at the edge of the moment
Heart pacing faster than time
Hands rehearsing calm in my pockets
While my breath betrayed me

For six years
You lived in pixels and promises
In late night calls and shared silences
In the spaces between what ifs
And maybe somedays

Now, you were here
Real
Walking toward me
Like a wish I was scared to want too much

My chest tightened, not from the air
But from the weight of wondering
"What if you don't like what you see?"
What if I fall harder
And you don't catch me

Your smile arrived before your footsteps did
And something inside me exhaled
But still, I was swimming nerves
Scared that the chemistry of the screen
Might not translate to the closeness of skin

I took you in like the sky after a storm
Hopeful, but still scanning for clouds
I wanted this
God, I wanted this

Your laugh cracked the fear
Your eyes softened the doubt
And every passing second felt like a hand
Pulling me closer to something that could grow

Possibility bloomed in the air with us
A slow and trembling bud
Reaching for the sun

I didn't know what we'd become
But for a fleeting heartbeat
I believed in love again
I saw futures
Folding into each other like pages
And I dared to dream
You might see them too

It wasn't electric
Unadorned
No fireworks kiss
No swelling music

Just your hand brushing mine
And not pulling away
Just your smile
Like you'd known all along

But to me
It was galaxies collapsing
Into a single, quiet breath

Masterpiece

She was not born, but breathed
A sigh exhaled from sacred space
Where silence dreamed of music's shape
And time stood still to see her face
The sky was canvas, void and waiting
Until her soul was brushed in flame
And when she stirred, the stars grew bashful
The night itself forgot its name

The moon spilled silver at her footsteps
The sea grew still to glimpse her eyes
And every god of myth and memory
Fell speechless under stormless skies
Aphrodite clawed the mirror
Venus cursed her own deceit
For mortal form had dared to wander
Past divine, and more complete

Her skin is made of ancient verses
Whispered once by dying kings
Her pulse, a rhythm, slow and holy
Beats like thunder wrapped in wings
The dawn delays for just a moment
To gild her hair in liquid gold
And dusk, too proud to dim her presence
Hangs the clouds in marbled folds

Each freckle, a star-mapped constellation
Each curve, a sculptor's final breath
Michelangelo would weep in shame
And trade his chisel in for death
She walks, and marble learns to soften
She speaks, and silence breaks apart
Not flesh and bone, but ether's daughter
An echo carved from bleeding art

No portrait frames what she embodies
No song contains the sound of *her*
The birds go mute in admiration
The wind forgets to stir
The roses bloom, then bow before her
Their jealous thorns too dulled to sting
And even thorns, in her reflection
Would choose instead to crown a king

She is the storm the sky remembers
The hush that fills a chapel's dome
The flame that dances in a mirror
But makes the mirror feel like home
A thousand poems fall beside her
Each line a feathered, broken plea
For ink may trace the outline's shadow
But never reach the melody

And I, a vagrant soul who saw her
Not with eyes, but something more
Who felt her presence like a haunting
I'd been unconsciously searching for
Now write in vain, though I am willing
To bleed until the letters cease
But still, no word can hold her essence
For she is
A Masterpiece

Already Yours

You never asked me to be
But I was

Somewhere between a shared laugh
And the way your voice softened when you spoke my name
I gave myself to you
In small, quiet ways

In the way I held your silence
Like a secret meant for two
Or how I traced the lines of your smile
When no one else would stay

I didn't need a label yet
You didn't need to claim me
My heart moved
Before my mind caught up

I was anticipating your texts already
Before you even hit send
Already learning your moods like the weather
Predicting the storms before they came

I would've followed you anywhere
And called it home
So long as your voice was at the other end

It wasn't a choice
Not really
It was a quiet becoming
A falling, without the crash

And by the time I realized how far I'd gone
I wasn't scared
I was still

Because I was already yours
Long before either of us
Knew what that meant

A Love So Divine

Six years of words, of dreams, of time
Our souls connected in rhythm and rhyme
The day we met, my heart did soar
For in your smile, I found something more

Your kindness, like a gentle breeze
Whispers in my heart, puts me at ease
A beauty that no earthly gaze could claim
A love that makes me question Thy name

Your eyes, a green so deep and bright
A sea of wonder, a guiding light
In them, I could lose myself for days
Drowned in their depths, lost in their gaze

I've never believed in all things divine
But in your eyes, I see a sign
For only God could create a soul so pure
A heart so open, love so sure

So here I stand, with hope in my chest
Waiting, wondering what is best
I'd follow you, wherever you go
For in your love, I sense, something, I don't know

The Wizard

There's a story told of a wizard
Who for money, would cast a spell
I'm sure that you met this wizard
And to you, his wares he did sell

For what else can explain how your smile
Can make my heartbeat roar
Or how your look slows my breathing
While causing my spirits to soar

I'm sure that you and this wizard
Conspired to control my brain
For I'm always thinking about you
Feeling happy and slightly insane

Now I hope I meet that same wizard
For I'd give him all of my gold
To make you want to stay with me
And share happiness as we grow old

Tiger Lily

She's the kind of beautiful
That doesn't chase attention
It blooms
Quiet and sudden
Like Tiger Lillies in a forgotten field

There's something in her eyes
Green like deep woods after rain
Where every glance
Feels like a secret unfolding

Her lips don't just speak
They sing
Soft as dusk
Full of stories I'd beg to hear twice

And when she smiles
The whole world leans in
Just to listen

She moves like a myth
Grace in every step
Fire in her frame
Not built for pedestals
But poetry

She's sharp without cutting
Funny without trying
Wise in ways that silence you

She finds joy in the cracks
And love in the overlooked
Then gives both away
Like they never cost her a thing

Kindness lives in her
Not as a mask
But as marrow
Even the wind slows down
Just to feel her pass

She doesn't just exist
She shifts the room
Softens the air
Makes everything
A little more possible

My Tiger Lily
Vivid, fierce,
And utterly unforgettable

There are people you don't just fall for.
You dissolve into them.
Every word, every glance, feels like home
you didn't know you were looking for.

Quiet Realizations

It didn't hit me all at once
Not like a crash
Or even thunder
More like a sunrise
Slow... quiet
Undeniable once it was there

I started noticing the little things
How I'd wait for your name to light up my phone
How your laughter lingered long after the call ended
I'd collect stories like souvenirs, just to hand them to you first

I started counting time
By when we last spoke
By when I'd hear from you next
You were becoming my rhythm
And I didn't realize I'd been offbeat
Until you

You made ordinary moments feel golden
Talking about what we'd name our future cats
Arguing over pizza toppings
Planning a trip we hadn't booked
But already believed in

I don't know when I stopped thinking
"I hope she stays around"
And starting thinking
"God, I want her to stay forever"

You weren't just someone I talked to
You were home
And every time we said goodnight
Forever sat on the tip of my tongue
Yours, if you wanted it

Yellow

Yellow is rare
Not like green
Rooted, endless, expected
Not like blue
Wide, still, indifferent
Not like brown or red
Earthy, steady, fading into the scene

But yellow?
Yellow interrupts
Yellow wildflowers in a green field make you look again
Make you slow down
Sometimes, they make you stop

I loved her yellow
The way she didn't try to be seen
But was
Effortlessly
Undeniably
Rare

Crazy

"Crazy!"
That's what we say
When the world makes no sense, But we're okay
When your smile flips my whole day around
And laughter is louder than any sound

It's in the way we finish each thought
In every wild twist that love has brought
No script, no rules, just sparks that fly
You and me, and the reason why

We chase the moon with hearts on fire
Built from chaos and sweet desire
Every look, every stolen kiss
Feels like falling and flying in perfect bliss

"Crazy!"
It's our secret code, our song
The word we've made our own all along
And if love like this is mad and free
Then *crazy* is exactly what I want to be

Crazy!

A Prayer

God, I want her to stay forever
Like sunlight, soft that warms the day
A steady light that doesn't dim
And never fades away

I want her voice, a gentle tune
To fill the spaces in my mind
A song beneath the silver moon
A melody that's sweet and kind

I want her smile, a tender flame
To brighten all my darkest skies
A quiet warmth that knows my name
And lifts my heart where true love lies

God, I want her to stay forever
not just in this moment's grace
But in each dawn and every ever
In every breath, and every place

I want her laughter, light as air
To dance like leaves upon the breeze
A joyful sound beyond compare
That sets my soul completely free

I want her hand, forever near
To hold and never let it go
Our fingers speak what hearts hold dear
In quiet love that only grows

God, let her stay in every sunrise
In every quiet night
In every laugh that fills the silence
In every part of my life

Where love lives
Where forever begins

Amen

She was never mine to frame
Only to stand before in quiet awe
Breathing her in as one does the ocean
Knowing the tide would always pull her away

Wake Of A Masterpiece

The canvas hangs, but now it weeps
A hollow where her colors bled
The strokes undone by time's erasure
The gold now rust, the roses dead

I walk the halls of memory
Where once her footsteps graced the floor
But echoes fade in fractured silence
A gallery behind locked doors

She was a flame that shamed the torches
A storm that taught the sky to cry
A painting hung in God's own chambers
That I could never justify

She smiled, and daylight lost its purpose
She spoke, and planets dared to shift
But I, a thief in awe of treasure
Could only touch, then watch it drift

What do you do, when art stops breathing?
When awe dissolves to phantom ache?
When all that held the stars together
Was one girl's shadow in your wake?

I kissed her once, too soft, too mortal
Like touching marble with regret
Her name still haunts my quiet mornings
A hymn the sun cannot forget

Now nothing stirs the same within me
No shape, no sound, no face compares
I live among imperfect portraits
In empty rooms and vacant stares

She is the brushstroke time can't capture
The echo I will always chase
My fingers ache to feel her outline
In every void, in every place

She was the poem I could not finish
The final verse I failed to keep
And now I walk through waking hours
In the cathedral of my grief

Almost

You ever watch someone hold your heart
Like it's a maybe?

It's like standing in the doorway
With the light spilling in
But never being asked inside

Like your name on their lips
But never their heart
Like fingertips that hover
But never hold

You get the warmth
But not the fire
The glances
But not the gaze
The words
God, the words...
But never the weight behind them

They almost choose you
Almost reach for you
Almost stay

And you learn
How to measure happiness in maybes
And heartbreak
In the silence between texts

You tell yourself
"This is close enough"
That maybe if you're patient
They'll love you fully someday
But someday isn't a promise
It's a soft letdown
Wrapped in hope

To almost be loved
Is to bleed quietly
From a wound that no one can see
To smile like it doesn't ache
To dance on the edge
Of something real
But always
Always
Alone

I Stayed

She broke me
Softly
With kindness in her voice
And guilt in her eyes

Said, "I can't be what you need"
And I nodded
Like I hadn't already built my whole world around her name

She didn't leave through a door
Just out of the us I thought we were still building

And I?
I remained
Not because I had to
But because I still cared
Because losing her completely felt heavier
Than carrying this quiet ache beside her

Now I smile through glass
Watch her laugh at jokes I wish I told
Give her comfort when my soul's on fire
I'm her friend...
But only on the outside

On the inside
I'm a graveyard of what ifs
A museum of almosts
A battlefield where every "I'm okay"
Is a lie I rehearse just to survive the way she says
"I'm grateful for you"

She says it like I'm strong
Like I'm noble
Like I'm not breaking in the exact shape of her silhouette

But I chose this
I chose to stay
Not because I'm brave
But because walking away
Felt like dying twice

A Little Bit Yours

You're not mine anymore
Not like before
But you're still here, in small familiar ways
A laugh
A glance
A moment caught by chance

We don't hold hands through storms now
But we still speak
Still reach across the space between

No late night calls
No whispered plans
But your voice still settles me
Still knows where to land

The chapter turned
I know that
Still, I trace the margins with careful fingers
Grateful, for the part that stayed

We've learned to care without the claim
To hold space without the weight
But even now, and forever more

I'm still, just a little bit yours.

Still It Happened

It's been 2 weeks
Since you broke my heart in two
And you didn't mean to, I know that
But still... it happened

Like a glass slipping slow in motion off the counter
You looked sorry before I even hit the ground
Your eyes held apology
But your mouth let loose a sentence
That sounded like Goodbye
And now every clock I look at ticks louder
Like it's mocking the silence you left behind

I rehearse your voice like a voicemail
I'm too scared to delete
There's comfort in the playback, but pain in the pause
Because no matter how many times I hit "replay"
You still walk away at the end

It's been 2 weeks
Long enough for the flowers I got you to wilt
And friends to stop asking "Are you okay?"
Long enough for me to smile in public
And cry when no one's around

You didn't mean too, I know
You said it like you stepped on my soul by accident
Like heartbreak was a spill you'd mop up and forget
But still... it happened

Still, I walk around carrying phantom conversation and
unfinished hugs
Still, I check my phone like it owes me closure
Still, I argue with the mirror about whether it was love or
convenience

And I hate that I defend you
In the courtroom of my own mind
"Guilty," I say
"But with good intentions," I add
Like that erases the ache
Like that uncracks the bone

It's been 2 weeks
And I still flinch when I see your name
In old playlists
In old group chats
In dreams I didn't mean to have

You didn't mean to
But that doesn't mean you didn't
And maybe that's the hardest part
Because even if the wound was carved by accident
I'm still the one bleeding

Still...
It happened

Tattooed Heart

Your name is tattooed on my heart
Carved with a knife
Inked in blood
No need for vows, no sacred art
Just pain that I mistook for love

It bleeds when I remember you
It burns when I pretend I don't
But I'd carve it deeper if I knew
You'd feel a fraction of this want

A haunted kind of tenderness
A love that tastes like iron and ash
But I still kiss the phantom wound
And trace your name
Beneath its gash

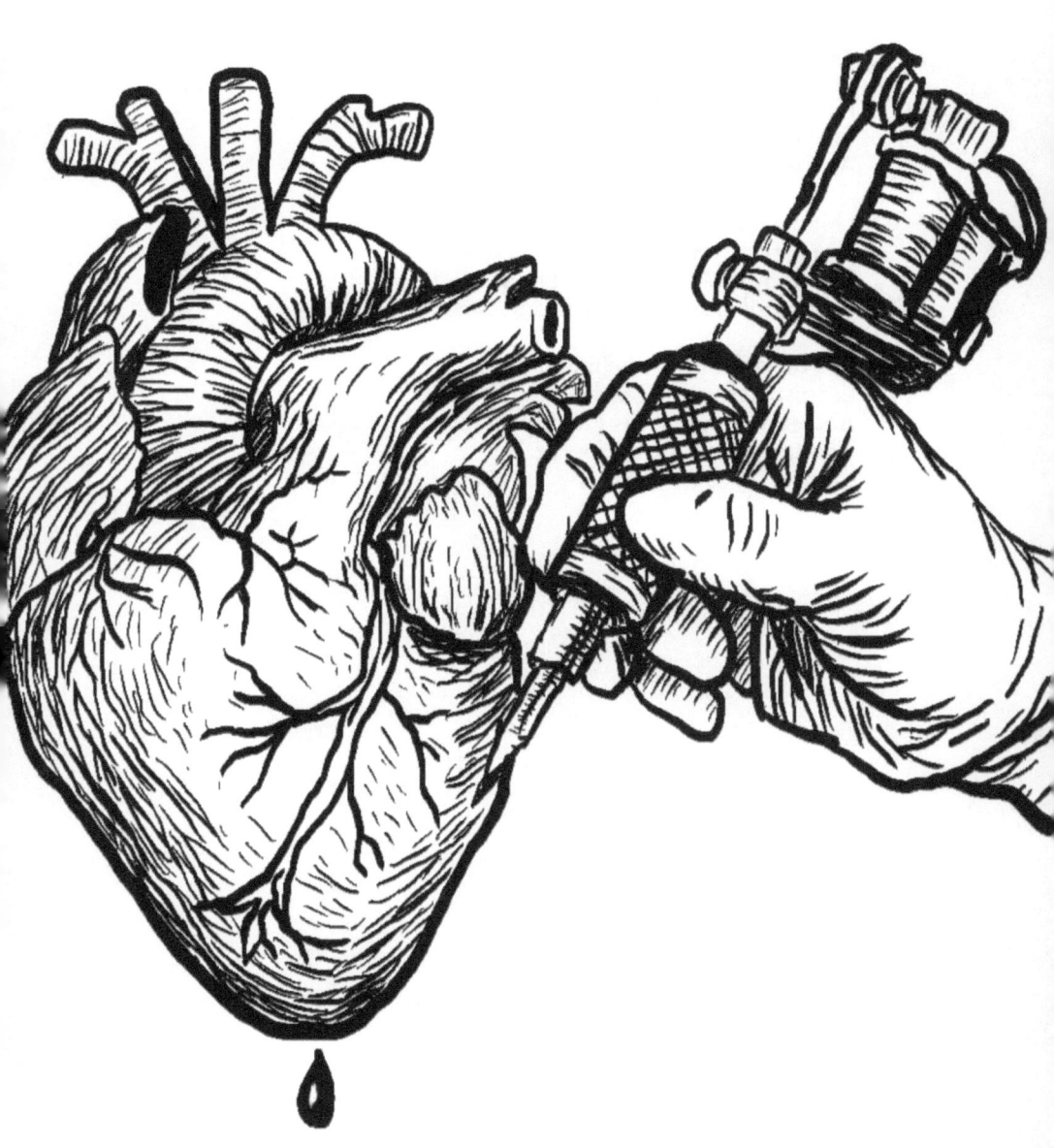

"Good night, Sleep well"

I told her, "Goodnight, Sleep well"
Like that was all I had to tell
Like I didn't reread our thread
And wonder where her warmth had fled

I bit my tongue on what was true
The part that whispered, "I miss you"
We barely spoke, but still I stayed
Hoping silence meant she hadn't swayed

So I tucked the ache behind my grin
Let distance wear a gentle skin
And gave her peace instead of pain
Though part of me felt lost again

Glass Smile

I laugh like glass that doesn't crack
With every joke, I take it back
The silence, screams I never said
The love that died but won't stay dead

You left so soft, No slammed front door
Just, "Take care now," and nothing more
I nodded like it meant no pain
And let you walk out in the rain

My friends still ask, "You doing fine?"
I pour out lies like vintage wine
"A clean break, yeah. Just wasn't right."□
Then sob through songs alone at night

I wear this mask that doesn't slip
Each smile rehearsed, each tightened grip
While deep beneath this calm disguise
A thousand tears behind my eyes

So here I stand, both whole and torn
A perfect face for love that's worn
And no one knows what's really true
Not even me. Not without you

I Lied

I didn't choose this
Let's get that straight
This wasn't mutual
Wasn't a handshake over coffee
Wasn't two people nodding
Like we both read the same page and decided to close the book

No
You ended the chapter
While I was still underlining sentences
Still memorizing your voice like it was a gospel
Still dreaming in our language

You said, "Lets just be friends"
I smiled like I understood
Like my heart didn't drop like a glass on tile

I didn't want this
I wanted US
All the mess and magic
The late night jokes
The small glances that said "I see you" without saying a word

You said we'd be better as friends
And I wonder... For who?
Because this doesn't feel better
It feels like tearing off a limb and framing it like art
Like calling a ghost a guest
Like asking me to stay in the house we built
But sleep in the attic
Alone

You want me near, but not too close
Just far enough to miss the most
From love to friend
From we to was
From maybe to never again

And I'll try
God, I'll try
To stand next to you and smile like it doesn't hurt
To laugh without wishing I could hold your hand through it

But please know... This isn't peace for me
This is surrender
This is silence in the shape of your goodbye

I didn't want this
But I'll carry it
Because loving you meant giving you what you needed
Even if it broke everything
I was still hoping for

So I'll smile when I see you
I'll stand by your side
But just know, everytime I say
"I'm okay"
I lied

A broken person made me break
I caught their falling pieces
But cut myself on every edge
I bled trying to hold them whole
Now I'm scattered in their place

More Than This

You drew a line, I rubbed it out
Hoping love could come about
You stepped with care, unsure, unclear
I followed close, then disappeared

In dreams I held a different truth
One painted in the shades of youth
I thought that maybe time would show
A path beyond the friend I know

But I mistook your gentle grace
As something more I had to chase
I leaned too far, I asked too much
From hands that offered only touch

You never promised more than this
I filled the space with what I wished
And now I see, it wasn't fair
To place my hopes in what wasn't there

You set a boundary, soft but true
And I kept reaching out for you
I blurred the lines, ignored the signs
The fault is quietly, fully mine

And if our bond can still remain
Untouched by pressure, free from strain
Then I will learn to just be near
Without the weight of want or fear

Still Saying Good Night

I told her, "Good night, sleep well"
Like we were still us
Like the word *friend*
Wasn't just a faded label
Barely sticking to the mess we became

She said we could still talk
Said, "I still care"
But care shouldn't feel this...
Distant
This quiet
This one sided

And I get it
We broke up
The kind of break where your heart doesn't shatter
It just... unplugs

But I stayed
Not because I'm stuck
But because I meant it
When I said *forever*
Even if forever shifted shape

I told her, "Good night, sleep well"
And hoped she'd say more than, "You too"
Hoped she'd remember
How I used to be her safe place
Not just another voice she scrolls past
When life gets too loud

You said we'd still be close
But your silence screams louder
Than the break up did

And me?
I'm here
Still typing out check ins
Like they're life lines
Still showing up to a friendship
That might've been a promise
You never planned to keep

But I told her, "Good night"
Because I don't know how to say
"I miss being important to you"
Without sounding like I'm asking
For more than I was left with

And maybe I am
Maybe I still want the version of you
Who once fought to stay in my life

But for now
I'll keep showing up
Keep hoping
Keep whispering
"Good night, sleep well"
To someone who already said
"Goodbye"

Roses

I mistook you for sunflowers
Bright, gentle,
Soft in sunlight
Growing in the wild, forgiving places

But you turned out to be roses
Elegant, yes
But wholly made of thorns

I reached for your bloom
Hands trembling
Believing beauty meant safety
That love would mean mercy

You never warned me
Never meant to hurt me
But still, I bled
A quiet price for closeness

I watered you
With pieces of myself
Let your silence wrap around me
Like choking vines

You never promised to stay
But I let myself believe it

Even now
I still find you beautiful
But I've learned not to touch the thorns

Unbound

It's strange how closeness fades away
How something bright begins to dim
A steady light that slips to gray
A sacred song turned distant hymn

Your name still lingers in the air
In quiet rooms and softened skies
A laugh I hear but cannot share
A truth I search for in goodbyes

No storm, no fire, no final sound
Just silence thick enough to feel
The way two hearts, once tightly bound
Begin to drift, begin to heal

I talked to God about you once
And I don't even completely believe
But still I asked, in fragile hopes
For something gentle to receive

Not answers, just the kind of peace
That doesn't ask for much to stay
A way to keep what had to cease
A grace to slowly walk away

Now time moves on without a pause
The days reshaped, the ties undone
But still I ache, without a cause
For all the ways we were once one

White Suit

I wore white today
Not for purity
But for protection

Blew dust from old machines
And let it cling to me instead
Every filter emptied
Felt like something else inside
Being wrung out too

sent her a photo

No caption could carry
How tired I looked
Beneath the mask

She said she was tired too

And that was it

No soft reach across the hour
No echo of a smile
Just
Quiet

I told her I hoped her day went well
She told me what she cleaned

I think she's still cleaning...
But not the kind of mess
That white suits are made for...

Borrowed Book

You were never mine
You were just a borrowed book
Pages worn soft by someone else's fingers
Margin notes written in a voice I couldn't erase

I read you slow
Careful not to fall too deep between the lines
Tried not to dog-ear the moments
That made my heart pause
Or underline the way you said my name

But you smelled like home
Faint lavender and longing
And I forgot you had a return date
Stamped somewhere in ink I didn't see

Still, I held you close at night
Whispered wishes into your spine
Pretending stories don't end
Even as the last chapter got closer
With every passing sigh

You were never mine
But I loved you like first editions
Like secrets sealed in parchment
Like maybe if I loved you gently enough
You'd stay

But you were just a borrowed book
And some endings are already written

Spoiled

I already know how this ends
Not just with heartbreak
But with silence

Not just goodbye...
But a slow unravelling...
Texts stop arriving
Calls I stop trying to make

She won't hate me
She'll just disappear
Because one day
Someone else will appear

He won't like her past
Won't like my name in her phone
Won't understand
That I was never just "someone before"

And she'll say it gently...
Or maybe not at all
Maybe I'll just feel it

The distance
The space where we used to be

But still...
I keep turning the pages

Because this middle?
This chapter of near-closeness
Of laughing like it's still then
Of her saying "hi" at 6 a.m...□
It matters to me

Even if it's all just a soft rewind
Before the real ending begins

Even if it's a countdown

I love her.□
And I'd rather read every line
Soak up the parts where she still lets me in
Than pretend the ending hasn't already been written

The story is spoiled
I'll lose her
Not to a fight
But to time
And timing
And someone else's arms

Still...
I'd rather stay in this chapter
Than close the book

Because the pages between
Are where *she* lives

I wandered halls of painted hearts,
Searching brushstrokes for the curve of her smile,
And shadowed corners for the light in her eyes,
But every frame was missing the one thing I came
for...
Her

The Gallery

I walked through rooms of quiet wonders
Canvases breathing in muted hues
Portraits of joy, of storms, of lovers
Lit by the hush of well placed truth

Each frame hung still with eager posture
As if to ask, "Could I be her?"
But none contained the pulse, the thunder
None caught the way her silence stirred

A woman's smile in oil and amber
Drew a breath, but not the kind
She used to steal with just a glance
Or by the way her hands aligned

A sketch of grace, a brush of longing
One piece wept blue across the glass
But even sorrow, dressed in beauty
Looked artificial as I passed

They tried
Oh, how they tried, those artists
With aching hands and fevered eyes
But she had something they lacked wholly:
A soul that beauty couldn't hide

In every corner, light bent wrongly
The shadows whispered half her name
I found no color deep enough
To paint the echo she became

And so I wandered, hungry, haunted
Searching in strokes for something more
But every wall became a mirror
That led me back to her once more

She is the piece they'll never capture
The gallery no hand could own
And I, just one more passing viewer
Pretending not to be alone

Cracked

It's been a little over a month
Since you dropped my heart like it was burning your hands
And maybe it was
Maybe I was too much fire
Too much weight
Too much love
Wrapped in softness you didn't know how to unwrap

You said, "Let's be friends"
And I smiled
Like that didn't feel like a funeral with no body to bury
Just a heartbeat echoing in a room you left behind

I'm hurting
But, I'm okay
And that's the weirdest part
Like, my chest is a cracked open window
Letting in all the wrong weather
But I'm still standing in it like it's summer

Still laughing at things
Still breathing
Even when my lungs whisper your name on the exhale
Still getting out of bed
Though your ghost has squatters rights on my pillow

I saw your smile in a stranger and didn't flinch
That's new
I wrote your name without cursing it
That's progress

I'm not broken
I'm breaking
In slow, careful pieces
That know how to find their way back

So yeah, It's been a little over a month
But time's a strange kind of glue
And I may be cracked...
But not all the way through

Her Own Flowers

She buys her own flowers now
Bright and full, arranged with care
The kind I used to bring her
Every other weekend
Like offerings

Back when love looked like

A three hour drive
And a fistful of fresh lilies
When her smile bloomed
Before she even saw what I held

Now she holds the vase with both hands
Showing me through a screen
Light spilling across her face
Like it used to when I walked through the door

She says she missed the color
Missed how it filled the house
How it softened the quiet
So she brought it back herself

And I smile, because
What else do you do
When the thing you planted still grows
Just not in your hands anymore?

She buys her own flowers now
And I pretend not to notice
That they look
Just like the kind I used to bring

Just A Memory

You're just a memory now
That's what I tell myself
Like it's something I can file away
Something that fits neatly in the past

But then I remember
your laugh
The way it filled a room
And settled into my bones

How your hair always smelled like lavender and fire
When you'd fall asleep beside me
As if the universe needed you to be soft and wild
All at once

I remember how your eyes lit up
When you spoke about things you loved
Sunsets, cats, the moon
How your voice would change
When you talked about the people you cared for

I remember your beautiful singing
Off tune, but fearless
Windows down
My heart trying not to show its grin
Oh, how I miss *your* sound

I remember being brave for the first time
Telling you I loved you
Not because it felt safe
But because it felt true

I remember silence too
Not the awkward kind
But the kind that holds hands with understanding
The kind you don't get back

You're just a memory now
That's the story I try to write
Try to live
But it never stays on the page

Because you will never be
JUST a memory to me now
You echo where I thought I was alone

The Breeze

I let the light in
Let the air move freely through the room
For a moment, everything felt lighter

But now, pages are scattered on the floor
Curtains tangled
Pieces of things I thought were secure lying where they shouldn't
be

How can I blame the wind for the mess it made
If it was me who opened the windows...
The breeze did feel nice for a little while though

I Don't Need To Move On

I don't need to move on
I don't want to
That's not what this is
I'm not trying to erase you,
Just trying not to disappear into the storm you've become

Because you are a volcano
Spitting fire in the middle of a hurricane
And I'm caught somewhere
Between drowning
And burning

Some days, you're warmth
Other days, you're ash in my lungs
And wind that tears at everything
I thought was solid

I never wanted to leave

I still don't
But I can't keep chasing you
Through earthquakes
And tidal waves
Calling it love just because I'm still standing

This isn't about letting go
It's about holding on
Without losing myself in the chaos
You can't seem to calm

I don't need to move on
I just need to survive without you
Without catching fire
Without sinking
Without forgetting
Who I am
When I'm not wrapped up
In you

Not Enough

I gave her everything I had
Every cracked piece of my heart
Every quiet word
Every steady step toward her

She said I was enough
More than enough
That my love was fierce
True, unshakable

But still, she left

Not because I faltered
Not because I failed
But because sometimes love
Isn't a question of giving
But of being what's wanted

And I am left standing
In the echo of her footsteps
Wondering how
To be enough
When all I ever wanted
Was to be enough for her

I did everything right
Held her when she broke
Loved her when she ran
Stayed when it hurt to stay

But still, it wasn't enough

So now I carry the weight
Of trying
Loving
Falling short

And learning, slowly
That sometimes
The hardest truth
Is that love alone
Is not always enough

The Echoes Between Us

I gave you every piece I had to give
A heart carved open, raw and wide
In every whispered hope I lived
Yet still, you slipped away inside

You said I did all right, you swear
But "right" was never quite enough
A shadow lingered in your air
A silent fault, a tender bluff

I held the space where friendship bloomed
Then watched it twist into a flame
A bittersweet and fragile tune
A love that neither could reclaim

You left me with these hollow rooms
Where echoes chase what used to be
I'm broken too, but I resume
The fight to mend what's left of me

No blame, no fury, just a sigh
For sometimes love's a cruel art
To try, to fall, to wonder why
We're never quite enough to start

Still, in the quiet, I remain
A witness to the love we lost
A bittersweet, enduring pain
A heart that bore the cost

I Showed Up

I woke up today
But my soul did not
My body moved
Out of habit, more than hope
A ghost wearing yesterday's skin
Pretending it still fits

The mirror said I'm alive
But the spark behind my eyes
Called me sick again
Maybe it's on strike
Maybe it's just hiding
Under a pile of unfinished dreams

Coffee helped me fake it
So did the playlist
So did the routine
That wears my name
But doesn't quite feel like mine yet

I answered messages
Laughed when I had to
Breathed because I must
But inside?
There was static
Like a radio stuck between stations
Like a scream
Under glass

Some days, surviving is sacred
Some days, being present
Is the best kind of poetry

So no
I didn't wake up whole today
But I showed up
And maybe
That's enough
For now

The Last Bag I'll Ever Pack

It's still sitting there,
that black backpack with the fraying zipper,
the one I packed a hundred times
with folded shirts and borrowed hope.

It was never just a bag.
It was a ritual,
a countdown to the next time
she'd open the door
and I'd step into the life
I thought we were building.

I used to pack it before I unpacked myself.
Before laundry,
before rest,
before anything...
because seeing her again
was always the next thing
worth living for

But today,
I dumped it out.

Not neatly.
Not with ceremony.
Just let it spill
like everything else she left behind.

A stray hoodie.□
A toothbrush.□
Cologne she liked the smell of.□
Things I didn't know
would one day become evidence
of something extinct.□

I thought today would be the day.□
Two months since the break.□
Almost three since I last saw her.□
I thought I'd unpack it for good,
a soft kind of closure,
a quiet surrender.□

But all it gave me
was the weight of goodbye
I'd been trying not to feel.□

Because when you stop packing,
you admit you're not going back.□
You admit she's not waiting.□
You admit the future you rehearsed
will never arrive.□

It's just a bag.□
But it used to mean everything.□
And now it's just
another thing I have to learn
to live without.

Walk Away

I want you to let me go
So I don't have to do it
So I don't have to carve
A goodbye out of something
That once felt like home

I want the door to close
From your side
So I can pretend I was just too late
Instead of too tired to keep knocking

I want your silence to speak first
So mine wont feel
Like a knife
In the shape of mercy

I want you
To turn your back gently
So I don't have to
Break
What I still love

So I don't have to walk away
With the weight
Of being
The one
Who did it

Can't Be Friends

I don't think we can be friends
Not like you imagined anyway
That would be turning us into something less special
And slightly more mundane

We are not a quiet whisper
Not a faded note in time
We are the echo of unspoken dreams
A rhythm, unscripted, sublime

To call this friendship feels too small
Like caging fire in my hands

You ask me to stay, to shrink this down
To fit inside your lines
But love can't wear a different name
And hearts don't realign

So let's not pretend, let's not rewrite
What we both know is true
If friends are all we'll ever be
Then I can't be that for you

The Risk I Took

The risk I took for you was calculated
But love was never part of the math
I traced the numbers, hesitated
Still, I followed down the path

I stood beside you, step for step
Through laughter, silence, highs and lows
I held on tight, the promise kept
Believing love was what it grows

I bet my heart, I rolled the dice
Convinced that time would make you see
But love won't bloom from sacrifice
If what you want is never me

You smiled at me, then walked away
No words to soften what I knew
I begged the stars, I wished you'd stay
But love won't stick when it's not true

I gave you all, but hearts don't trade
No debts to weigh, no dues to call
The risk I took for you was made
And in the end
I lost it all

The End

About The Author

Tyler Copple is a writer and illustrator whose work explores life in all its forms. From quiet introspective moments, to the rush of change and growth. He's been writing poetry since childhood, first picking up the craft around the age of twelve, and has carried it ever since.

This is his debut collection, but far from his last. Tyler plans to continue creating and publishing works that reflect the depth, humor, and beauty of everyday life.

When he's not writing or sketching, Tyler can usually be found fishing, gaming, or finding inspiration in the small moments that others might overlook.

Follow Tyler on Tiktok: @tcoppoetry

For business inquiries, contact: contact@tcopmedia.com